2016 Innocents Database Exoneration Report

By Hans Sherrer

2016 Innocents Database Exoneration Report

Copyright © 2017 by Hans Sherrer

Permission is granted to publish content in this report with the sole proviso that credit for the source must be given.

Published by:
The Justice Institute
PO Box 66291
Seattle, WA 98166

Website: http://justicedenied.org
Email: contact@justicedenied.org

March 20, 2017

Trade Paperback ISBN: 154480430X
Trade Paperback ISBN-13: 978-1544804309

The map of the United States on the cover uses colors for each state to represent the total number of known exonerations for each state through 2016. The map was created with Carto.com.

The Justice Institute's logo that represents the snake of evil and injustice climbing up to tilt the scales of justice, is in the lower left-hand corner of the cover.

Table of Contents

Introduction	1
Observations	3
Longest Time From Conviction To Judicial Exoneration	5
Longest Time From Conviction To Executive Exoneration	6
Longest Time From Commission Of Crime To Conviction	7
Table 1 — Known Exonerations By Year (U.S. & Int.)	9
Chart 1 — Exonerations By Year	9
Table 2 — Number of Exonerated People By State	10
Map 1 — U.S. Map of Total Exonerations for each State	11
Table 3 — Number of Exonerated People By Jurisdiction (U.S.)	11
Table 4 — Number of Exonerated People By Sex/Type (U.S.)	11
Table 5 — Number of Exonerated People By Type of Crime (U.S.)	12
Chart 2 — Percentage of Exonerations by type of Crime (U.S.)	12
Table 6 — Number of Exonerated People by Race/Ethnicity (U.S.)	12
Table 7 — Number of Exonerated People By Primary Types of Exculpatory Evidence (U.S.)	13
Table 8 — Number of Exonerated People By Conviction Method (U.S.)	13
Table 9 — Number of Exonerated People Convicted After More Than One Trial (U.S.)	13
Table 10 — Number of State Prisoners Exonerated After Federal Habeas Granted (U.S.)	13
Table 11 — Number of Exonerated People Convicted By Primary Types of Prosecution Evidence (U.S)	14
Table 12 — Number of Exonerated People By Method of Exoneration (U.S.)	14
Table 13 — Number of Exonerated Persons Involved In A Case With A Co-Defendant (U.S.)	14
Table 14 — Number of Exonerations Involving DNA Evidence By Year	15
Chart 3 — Exonerations Relying On DNA Evidence in the U.S. and Internationally	15
Chart 4 — Percentage of Exonerations based on DNA evidence – 1989-2006 (U.S.)	16
Table 15 — Number of Exonerated People Aided By Conviction Integrity Unit (U.S.)	16
Table 16 — Number of Exonerated People By Years In Custody (U.S.)	16
Table 17 — Average Years Exonerated Person Was In Custody Before Release (All types of cases)	17
Table 18 — Avg Years Exonerated Person Was In Custody Before Release (Homicide or Sexual Assault only)	17
Table 19 — Avg Years Exonerated Person Was In Custody Before Release (Non-Homicide or Sexual Assault only)	17
Chart 5 — Average Years in Custody Before Exoneration (U.S.)	17
Table 20 — Number of Exonerated People By County (12 or more) (U.S.)	18
Table 21 — Number of Exonerated People By Country – International Cases Only	19
Table 22 — Number of Exonerated People By Type of Crime (International)	21
Table 23 — Number of Exonerated People By Method of Exoneration (International)	21
Table 24 — Number of Exonerated Persons Involved In A Case With A Co-Defendant (International)	21
Map 2 — World Map of Total Exonerations for each Country	22
Federal Court Is The Death Zone For Innocent State Prisoners	23

A question, correction, or suggestion regarding the Innocents Database can be emailed to:
innocents@justicedenied.org

Introduction

This is the second yearly report of information recorded in the Innocents Database through the last calendar year – 2016.[1] The Innocents Database is an ongoing independent non-profit project begun in February 1997 that records every documentable exoneration in the United States and every other country.[2] The Innocents Database is online at www.justicedenied.org/exonerations.htm, and it can be accessed from Justice Denied's website at www.justicedenied.org. This Report is compiled from information available in the database online.[3]

The database includes 8,131 cases concluded through December 31, 2016: 5,224 U.S. cases and 2,907 international cases.

Since the Innocents Database was founded there has been a continuing increase in the reporting of cases in accessible digital form. That has resulted in more cases being included for recent years. However, that doesn't mean more people are exonerated today than ten, twenty, or even forty years ago. It does means it is easier to find a larger number of recent exoneration cases. For example, Table 1 lists 484 U.S. cases and 462 international cases for 2016, and 84 U.S. cases and 97 international cases for 2005. There may have been a comparable number of exonerations in 2005 as 2016 – but finding and identifying contemporary cases is less challenging than 2005 cases, much less cases in 1995 or 1975.

Nevertheless, the 5,224 U.S. cases listed in the database through 2016 – 4,313 cases from 1989 to 2016 and 911 cases prior to 1989 – provide data that can be useful to make general observations and identify possible trends. 1989 is used as a quasi demarcation because the first DNA exoneration in the U.S. was in 1989. Internationally the first exoneration was in Canada in 1992.

The Report includes 24 tables of data. Most of the 24 tables include information about U.S. cases for both the years 1989 to 2016, and pre-1989, and several include information about international cases. Those tables are:

- Table 1. Known Exonerations By Year (U.S. & Int.)
- Table 2. Number of Exonerated People By State
- Table 3. Number of Exonerated People By Jurisdiction (U.S.)
- Table 4. Number of Exonerated People By Sex/Type (U.S.)
- Table 5. Number of Exonerated People By Type of Crime (U.S.)
- Table 6. Number of Exonerated People by Race/Ethnicity (U.S.)
- Table 7. Number of Exonerated People By Primary Types of Exculpatory Evidence (U.S.)
- Table 8. Number of Exonerated People By Conviction Method (U.S.)
- Table 9. Number of Exonerated People Convicted After More Than One Trial (U.S.)
- Table 10. Number of State Prisoners Exonerated After Federal Habeas Granted (U.S.)
- Table 11. Number of Exonerated People Convicted By Primary Types of Prosecution Evidence (U.S.)
- Table 12. Number of Exonerated People By Method of Exoneration (U.S.)
- Table 13. Number of Exonerated Persons Involved In A Case With A Co-Defendant (U.S.)
- Table 14. Number of Exonerations Involving DNA Evidence By Year (U.S. & Int.)
- Table 15. Number of Exonerated People Aided By Conviction Integrity Unit (U.S.)
- Table 16. Number of Exonerated People By Years In Custody (U.S.)
- Table 17. Average Years Exonerated Person Was In Custody Before Release (U.S. & Int.)
- Table 18. Average Years Exonerated Person Was In Custody Before Release (<u>Homicide or Sexual Assault</u>

---

[1] This report includes cases that were concluded through December 31, 2016, and which were added to the database up to March 7, 2017. For an explanation of cases considered an exoneration for inclusion in the Innocents Database, see, Hans Sherrer, "An Exoneration Can Be Judicial Or By Executive Or Legislative Clemency," *Justice Denied*, Issue 59 (Spring 2015), available online at, http://justicedenied.org/wordpress/archives/2811. Summarized, an exoneration is when a convicted living or deceased person's presumption of innocence is restored by judicial, executive, or legislative action, or their conviction is recognized as a miscarriage of justice by either legislative or executive action based on evidence of their innocence.

[2] The Innocents Database was created and is maintained by Hans Sherrer, president of the Justice Institute, and publisher and editor of *Justice Denied: the magazine for the wrongly convicted*.

[3] The Innocents Database contains millions of bits of data. The database can be sorted and searched on over 100 fields online at, http://forejustice.org/exonerations.htm .

only) (U.S. & Int.)
- Table 19. Average Years Exonerated Person Was In Custody Before Release (<u>Non-Homicide or Sexual Assault only</u>) (U.S. & Int.)
- Table 20. Number of Exonerated People By County (12 or more) (U.S.)
- Table 21. Number of Exonerated People By Country – International Cases
- Table 22. Number of Exonerated People By Type of Crime (International)
- Table 23. Number of Exonerated People By Method of Exoneration (International)
- Table 24. Number of Exonerated Persons Involved In A Case With A Co-Defendant (International)

Observations

The following are observations regarding known exonerations in the United States in 2016. The data underlying these observations is in the tables in this report and the Innocents Database.

In 2016, there was an exoneration in all but nine states: Alabama; Alaska; Hawaii; Kentucky; New Hampshire; New Mexico; Rhode Island; South Dakota; and Vermont.

In 2016, eight states had 10 or more exonerations: Pennsylvania (150); Texas (134); New York (33); Illinois (19); Oregon (16); California (12); Virginia (12); and, Ohio (10).

Five counties had ten or more exonerations in 2016: Philadelphia County, Pennsylvania (146); Harris County, Texas (80); Cook County, Illinois (13); Cuyahoga County, Ohio (10); and, Deschutes County, Oregon (10).[4]

Four cities had ten or more exonerations in 2016: Philadelphia (146); Houston (22); New York City (17); Chicago (13).

In 2016, 92% of exonerations were of men, and 8% were of women. That was consistent with the historical average of 91% men and 9% women.

In 2016, 74% of exonerations involved a case in which no crime was committed.

In 2016, 26% of exonerations were by way of an acquittal, by either a court reviewing the person's conviction or after a retrial. The remaining exonerations were by way of the dismissal of charges. That is consistent with the historical average of 22% of exonerations in the U.S. by way of an acquittal.

In 2016, 8% of exonerated people had one or more co-defendants also wrongly convicted. That was less than half the historical average of 18% of exonerations involving two or more co-defendants.

In 2016, 53% of exonerations were of a drug related conviction; 18% were of a non-violent related conviction; 14% were of a homicide related conviction; and 7% were of sexual assault/abuse related conviction.

In 2016, no one was posthumously exonerated.

In 2016, 77% of exonerated persons spent less than a year in custody, or were sentenced to probation or a fine; 23% spent a year or more in custody; 11% spent 10 years or more in custody; 7% spent 20 years or more in custody; and one person spent more than 30 years in custody. That was Keith Allen Harward, convicted of the 1982 murder of the husband of a rape victim in Virginia, and who was released after more than 33 years in custody.

In 2016, 64% of exonerated people were convicted by a guilty or no-contest plea, 29% by a jury, and 7% after a bench (judge only) trial.

In 2016, 96% of exonerations were of a person convicted in state court, and 4% in federal court.

In 2016, 2.5% of exonerations involved a false confession by the exonerated person or a co-defendant. That is less than half the average for the ten years from 2007 to 2016 when more than 5% of exonerations involved a false confession, and less than one-third the historical average of 8%.

The average of 17 years spent in custody by people exonerated in 2016 of a homicide or sexual assault related crime was _seven times_ the average of 2½ years spent in custody by an exonerated person who was convicted of any other type of crime.

Other than the six women exonerated in 2016 of a homicide related crime, the women who were incarcerated for all other types of crimes spent an average of _less than nine months_ in custody.

In 2016, 3.5% of U.S. exonerations were primarily based on new DNA evidence. Although they get a lot of press coverage, DNA exonerations are uncommon. They accounted for less than 3% of exonerations from 2013 to 2016, and since the first DNA exoneration in 1989, 8.3% of exonerations in the U.S. – 1 out of 12 – were primarily based on DNA evidence.

---

[4] The only known exonerations in Deschutes County were the ten in 2016, so it isn't listed in Table 20 that only includes counties with 12 or more total exonerations.

Conviction integrity units in ten jurisdictions aided in the exoneration of 118 people in 2016. There were 79 in Harris County (Houston) Texas; eight in Cook County, Illinois; seven each in Bexar County, Texas and Cuyahoga County, Ohio; and 17 in six other counties. The 173 exonerations aided by the Harris County CIU from 2014 to 2016 are due to laboratory testing for the first time of evidence in drug cases that turned out not to be an illegal substance, or retroactive application of rulings in two cases in which the Texas Court of Criminal Appeals ruled the Texas statute relied on for the convictions was unconstitutional.[5] In contrast with the Harris County CIU acting as a pass-through for testing conducted by a crime lab and new court rulings, the 21 exonerations by the Kings County, New York CRU are attributable to serious reinvestigation of those cases by CRU personnel after District Attorney Kenneth Thompson took office in January 2014.[6]

In 2016, six state prisoners were exonerated after their federal habeas corpus petition was granted. That is comparable with the average of about four per year since enactment of the Anti-terrorism and Effective Death Penalty Act of 1996.[7] The difficulty of a state prisoner to prevail in federal court is emphasized by the small number of exonerations contrasted with the thousands of state prisoner habeas petitions filed annually in U.S. District Courts.[8] That puts to rest the folklore a state prisoner can expect to get a fairer shake in federal court than their state's courts. See page 23 of this report for the mini-report, *Federal Court Is The Death Zone For Innocent State Prisoners*.

In the U.S. there are over a million felony convictions yearly in state courts, and more than 125,000 convictions in federal courts, so even given only a 2% wrongful conviction rate – and there are estimates the actual rate is 10% or more – there would be more than 22,000 wrongful convictions per year.[9] So the 484 cases in the database for 2016 are little more than 2% of that number. What is unknown – and for the foreseeable future it will remain unknown – is exactly how many innocent people have had their wrongful conviction(s) overturned. Also unknown is the infinitely larger number of innocent people – possibly totaling over a million – who have not, and never will have their wrongful conviction(s) overturned: those people will forever be officially branded as a criminal for a crime committed by another person, or that may not have even occurred. Thus, the known exonerations are a miniscule representation of the actual number of wrongly convicted persons.

The inadequacy of current data regarding wrongful convictions is illustrated by the fact that even though far more Caucasians are convicted than any other "racial" group, 50% of the exonerations in 2016 were identified as being Blacks. From 2012 to 2016 46% of known exonerations were of a Black man or woman.

The following are observations regarding known exonerations in countries other than the United States in 2016. The data underlying these observations is in the tables in this report and the Innocents Database.

In 2016, there was an identifiable exoneration in 41 countries. That is comparable to the 39 countries with a known exoneration in 2015.

In 2016, eight countries had 10 or more exonerations: Turkey (275); India (32); United Kingdom (England) (25); Malawi (19); Australia (14); and, China (11).

In 2016, 91% of exonerations were of men, and 9% were of women. That was consistent with the historical average of 88% men and 12% women.

In 2016, 22% of exonerations involved a case in which no crime was committed.

---

[5] The two statutes involved online solicitation of a minor, and photographing people in public without consent.

[6] DA Thompson died of cancer at the age of 50 on October 9, 2016. It is unknown at this time if his predecessor will support the CRU as a mechanism to ferret out unreliable convictions, or revert to the approach of Thompson's predecessor Charles Hynes., that the CRU was effectively only a public relations prop.

[7] Also known as AEDPA, Pub. L. No. 104-132, 110 Stat. 1214. Signed into law by President Clinton on April 24, 1996.

[8] See, Judicial Facts and Figures 2015, Table 4.6. "U.S. District Courts – Prisoner Petition Filed, by Nature of Suit," USCourts.gov. Available online at, http://www.uscourts.gov/file/19692/download. (Last visited March 15, 2017) 2015 is the most recent year that the statistics are available.

[9] 850,365 defendants were convicted in federal court during the six years 2010 to 2015 – an average of 141,727 per year. See, U.S. Attorneys' Statistical Reports available online at, http://www.justice.gov/usao/resources/annual-statistical-reports (Last visited March 15, 2017). There were 1,132,290 felony convictions in state courts in 2006, the latest year for which the data is available from the Bureau of Justice Statistics. See, Sean Rosenmerkel, Matthew Durose and Donald Farole, Jr., Ph.D.; "Felony Sentences in State Courts, 2006 – Statistical Tables," *Bureau of Justice Statistics*, December 2009, NCJ 226846. Available online at, http://www.bjs.gov/content/pub/pdf/fssc06st.pdf (Last viewed March 15, 2017).

In 2016, 96% of exonerations were by way of an acquittal, by either a court reviewing the person's conviction or after a retrial. The remaining exonerations were by way of the dismissal of charges. That was higher than the historical average of 78% of exonerations outside the U.S. by way of an acquittal.

In 2016, 17% of exonerated people had co-defendants also wrongly convicted. That was about half the historical average of 33% of exonerations involving two or more co-defendants.

In 2016, 9% of exonerations were of a homicide related conviction, 4% were of sexual assault/abuse related conviction, 5% were of a fraud related conviction, 63% were of a violence related conviction other than homicide, rape, assault, robbery, etc., and 13% were of a non-violent related conviction. Less than 1% of exonerations were of a drug related conviction, contrasted with 53% in the U.S. in 2016.

In 2016, there were two posthumous exonerations internationally.

In 2016, seven people were exonerated after more than 20 years of imprisonment. The longest was the more than 23 years of imprisonment by Chen Man, who was convicted of a murder and arson in China he didn't commit. Four of the other seven people who served more than 20 years were also convicted in China, and the other two were convicted in Japan.

The average of 9 years spent in custody by people exonerated in 2016 of a homicide or sexual assault related crime was *six times* the average of 1½ years spent in custody by an exonerated person who was convicted of any other type of crime.

In 2016, Kengo Iwamoto in Japan was the only person whose exoneration was primarily based on new DNA evidence. There have been a total of 39 DNA exonerations outside the U.S. since Canadian David Milgaard was cleared of murder and rape in 1992. Twelve of those exonerations were in Canada, 10 in the United Kingdom (England), three in Indonesia, three in New Zealand, three in Japan, and eight in seven other countries.

The following are three notable U.S. 2016 exoneration cases: the longest time from conviction to a judicial exoneration; the longest time from conviction to an executive (pardon) exoneration; and the longest time from an exonerated person's conviction and the commission of the crime.

Longest Time From Conviction To Judicial Exoneration

52 years
Paul Gatling
Convicted in 1964. Exonerated in 2016
Kings County, New York

Paul Gatling was convicted in 1964 of the shooting murder of Lawrence Rothbort on the night of October 15, 1963 during an attempted robbery in his Brooklyn, New York home. Rothbort's wife Marlene told police a man entered their apartment and demanded money, and shot her husband when he refused to give him any money. She gave the police a description of the assailant.

Gatling, a decorated Korean War veteran, was questioned after the police were told he had been seen in the area of the apartment building. There was no physical or forensic evidence linking Gatling to the shooting. He was charged with first-degree murder based on his identification by the victim's wife, after she had first failed to identify him in a four person line-up.

The 29-year-old Gatling proclaimed his innocence and pled not guilty during his arraignment. However, during his trial the visibly pregnant Marlene pointed to him as the man who shot her husband. Facing a possible death sentence if he was convicted by the jury, Gatling's trial abruptly ended when he accepted the prosecution's offer to plead guilty to second-degree murder in exchange for a prison sentence.

Gatling had buyer's remorse about his guilty plea, but his motion to withdraw it was denied.

In October 1964 he was sentenced to 30 years to life in prison.

Legal Aid Society lawyer Malvina Nathanson took an interest in Gatling's case because of his insistence he was innocent. Her investigation led her to believe he was in fact innocent. In 1973 she submitted a clemency application on Gatling's behalf to New York Governor Nelson Rockefeller. In one of his last acts before leaving office on December 18, 1973, Rockefeller commuted Gatling's sentence.

Gatling was released in January 1974 after more than ten years in custody.

In January 2014 new Kings County District Attorney Kenneth Thompson took office. Gatling read that Thompson was planning to reinvigorate the DA Office's Conviction Review Unit that had been created in 2011 by Thompson's predecessor, DA Charles J. Hynes. However, under Hynes it had not contributed to the overturning of a single conviction.

Gatling contacted Nathanson. Although they had not been in contact for decades, she had kept her file about Gatling's case. She sent it to him, and he provided it to Eric Sonnenschein, one of ten assistant district attorneys that Thompson had assigned to the CRU.

The CRU initiated an investigation of Gatling's case. The investigation discovered that Gatling was not provided with a lawyer prior to being interrogated about the crime, and that prior to Gatling's guilty plea his lawyer had not been provided with favorable evidence known to the DA, as was required by the U.S. Supreme Court in *Brady v. Maryland* (1963).

The non-disclosed evidence included: immediately after the crime Marlene Rothbort described the assailant as younger than Gatling; the Rothbort's neighbors told the police the couple often had violent arguments — sometimes during the night; that Marlene told detectives she was having an affair with a musician, Leon Tolbert, who was living as a boarder in the Rothbort's home; and, that when Tolbert was interviewed he told the police he had recently heard Marlene threaten to kill her husband if he ever hit her again.

The CRU's report determined that Gatling's conviction was a miscarriage of justice, and recommended that the DA's Office support the withdrawal of Gatling's guilty plea and the setting aside of his conviction. DA Thompson agreed with the recommendation. The DA's Office filed a motion for withdrawal of Gatling's guilty plea and to set-aside his conviction. On May 2, 2016 Brooklyn Supreme Court Justice Dineen Riviezzo granted the DA's motion, and also granted the DA's motion to dismiss the charge against the 81-year-old Gatling.

Thompson told reporters: "Paul Gatling repeatedly proclaimed his innocence even as he faced the death penalty back in the 60s. He was pressured to plead guilty and, sadly, did not receive a fair trial."[10]

After the hearing that cleared him almost 52 years after his conviction, Gatling told reporters that Marlene Rothborts' testimony doomed him: "The cops told me they would make sure I was convicted and the lawyers said they were going to execute me. I was a young black man. With the white, pregnant wife in front of an all-white jury pointing me out, it was over."[11]

Longest Time From Conviction To Executive Exoneration

24 years
Earnest Leap
Convicted in 1992. Exonerated in 2016
Jackson County, Missouri

In 1989 Earnest Leap was 31 and living in Jackson County, Missouri. He had primary custody of his two sons, five-year-old Brodie and his toddler brother Josh, that he had with his ex-wife Karen.

Leap and Karen were divorced in September 1989. She was displeased he was granted primary custody of their sons, which meant they spent more time with Leap than with her. Although there had never been any allegation by anyone that Leap had abused Brodie, on December 1, 1989 Karen quizzed Brodie, "Have you been

---

[10] "Man, 81, who served 10 years for 1960s New York murder he did not commit is finally cleared of his crime," By Mia De Graff, *Daily Mail*, May 2, 2016. Online at, http://www.dailymail.co.uk/news/article-3570129/Man-81-served-10-years-1960s-New-York-murder-did-not-commit-finally-cleared-crime.html .
[11] "Man Convicted of Brooklyn Murder Exonerated After 52 Years," by Dan Slepian and Corky Siemaszko, NBCNews.com, May 2, 2016. Online at, http://www.nbcnews.com/news/us-news/man-convicted-brooklyn-murder-exonerated-after-52-years-n566076 .

touched down there?"[12] Brodie said "No." She kept asking him again and again, and he finally told her "Yes."

Based on Brodie's statement Karen went to the police and asserted that Leap had fondled his son's genitals.

Leap was charged with criminal sexual assault. After insisting on his innocence for three years, to avoid Brodie having to testify at a trial, he took his lawyer's advice to agree to an Alford plea in exchange for probation. Under the deal Leap's conviction would be expunged after three years of good behavior. At the time Missouri did not have a sex offender registration law.

In 1994 a federal law was enacted creating a public sex offender registry in each state. So a year before he expected to have his conviction erased, Leap was required to register – and be publicly identified – as a child sex offender.

Eighteen years after accusing his dad of sexually touching him, Brodie recanted his claim in 2007. He asserted in an Affidavit that his mother pressured him into falsely accusing his father because she was angry he had been granted primary custody of him and his younger brother.

In 2015, the 57-year-old Leap retired as a driver for United Parcel Service. Brodie, who was a Navy veteran, moved in with his dad to help with his mission of being granted a pardon and clearing his name. In an October 2015 interview with *The Kansas City Star*, Brodie said about his false accusation, "I live with the guilt of that lie every day of my life." Brodie's brother Josh said about his dad, "The only stable component of my childhood was the immutable presence of my father."[13]

Missouri State Representative Jim Neely saw the story in *The Kansas City Star*, and became an advocate for Leap. In May 2016 Neely delivered a letter to Missouri Governor Jay Nixon in support of a pardon for Leap, which was signed by more than a third of Missouri House representatives.

On August 19, 2016 Governor Nixon signed Leap's pardon. Nixon stated: "The executive power to grant clemency is one I take with a great deal of consideration and seriousness. ... the information that has come to light more recently and the fact that he has been a law-abiding and productive member of society were compelling enough for me to grant a pardon."[14]

Longest Time From Commission Of Crime To Conviction

55 years
Jack McCullough
Crime occurred in 1957. Convicted in 2012. Exonerated in 2016
DeKalb County, Illinois

Jack McCullough was 72 when he was convicted on September 12, 2012 of the cold-case abduction of 7-year-old Maria Ridulph in Sycamore, Illinois on the evening of December 3, 1957 and her murder. Ridulph's body was found five months later in 1958.

At the time of Ridulph's murder McCullough was 18 and living in Sycamore. McCullough was questioned by police, and he told them that on the evening of Ridulph's disappearance he was in Rockford, Illinois. Rockford is 42 miles from Sycamore.

Fifty-four years later, in 2011, McCullough was living in Washington state when he was charged with Ridulph's murder. He was extradited to Illinois. McCullough's prosecution was based on circumstantial evidence that included alleged admissions he had made that suggested he was involved – but he did not confess and adamantly denied he abducted and killed Ridulph.

McCullough waived his right to a jury trial. After McCullough's conviction by Kane County Associate Judge

---

[12] "'Lie' begets lifetime of regret for Clay County father, son," By Eric Adler, *The Kansas City Star*, October 24, 2015. Online at, http://www.kansascity.com/news/local/article41364675.html .
[13] *Id.*
[14] "Decades after 'lie' puts dad on sex offender registry, he's pardoned," By Eric Adler, *The Kansas City Star*, August 19, 2016. Online at, http://www.kansascity.com/news/local/article96788667.html .

James Hallock following a bench trial, he was sentenced to life in prison.

DeKalb County State's Attorney Richard Schmack took office in 2013. McCullough was in the process of appealing his conviction. McCullough initially opposed McCullough's direct appeal. However, Schmack began having doubts when he reviewed the case, including police reports from 1957 and '58 that Judge Hallock had excluded from consideration as evidence during McCullough's trial.

Schmack reopened McCullough's case, and the investigation discovered the new evidence of phone records that corroborated McCullough's alibi that at the exact time Maria Ridulph was abducted in Sycamore, he was 42 miles away in Rockford.

Based on the reinvestigation, Schmack publicly proclaimed that McCullough was factually innocent and had been wrongly convicted.

On April 15, 2015 DeKalb County Judge William Brady granted a motion by the DeKalb County State's Attorney's Office to vacate McCullough's conviction. The motion was based on evidence of McCullough's actual innocence not considered by Judge Hallock in finding him guilty.

Judge Brady ordered McCullough's release on bond, and two hours later he was released from the DeKalb County Jail.

On April 22, 2016 Judge Brady granted a motion by the State's Attorney's Office to dismiss the murder charge against McCullough.

| Table 1 — Known Exonerations By Year (U.S. & Int.) ||||
Year	USA	Posthumous	International	Posthumous
2016	484	0	462	2
2015	721	4	211	2
2014	351	4	208	1
2013	206	4	189	0
2012	149	0	142	2
2011	131	2	161	1
2010	333	0	96	0
2009	158	3	155	3
2008	135	0	163	0
2007	142	28	172	8
2006	175	80	114	3
2005	84	0	97	1
2004	93	0	139	0
2003	127	2	74	3
2002	92	1	50	2
2001	106	1	50	0
2000	257	2	33	0
1999	62	0	27	0
1998	49	0	34	4
1997	57	0	15	0
1996	60	1	8	0
1995	85	0	19	0
1994	44	0	10	0
1993	46	0	10	0
1992	43	0	18	0
1991	50	0	12	0
1990	39	0	5	0
1989	34	1	13	0
1989-2016 total	4313	133	2687	32
<1989 total	911	27	220	34
Total	5224	160	2907	66

Chart 1 — Exonerations By Year

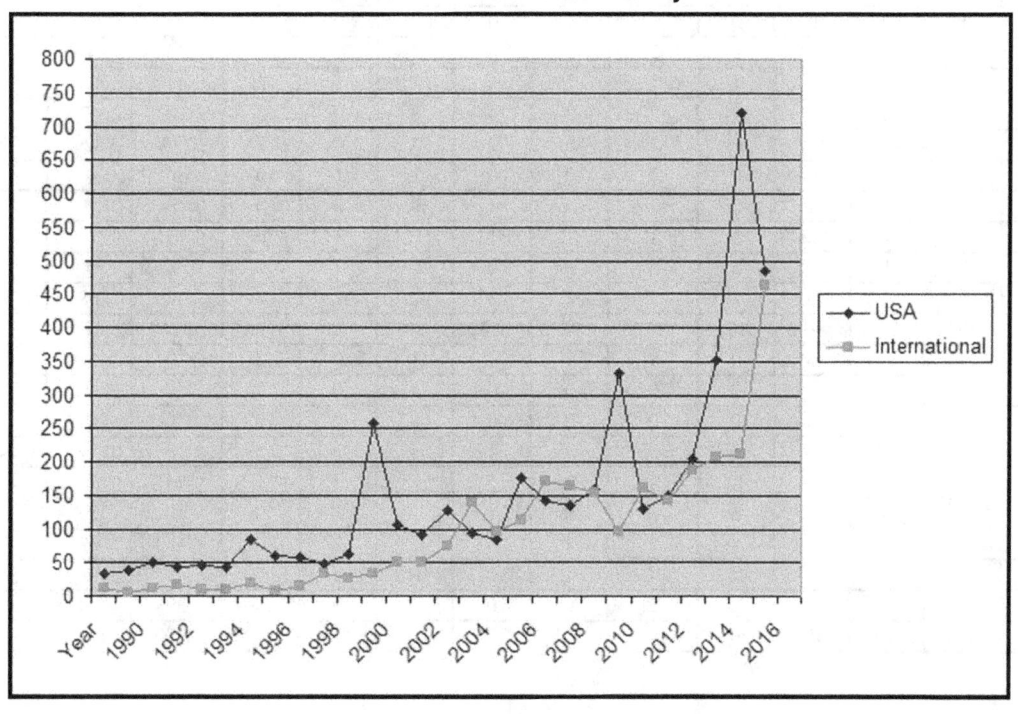

Table 2 — Number of Exonerated People By State														
State/Territory	2016	2015	2014	2013	2012	2011	2010	2009	2008	2007	10 yr total	1989-2016	Pre-1989	Total
Alabama	0	5	1	3	2	2	0	1	0	0	14	40	18	58
Alaska	0	6	1	0	1	0	0	0	0	0	8	9	3	12
Arizona	1	1	1	1	4	0	3	1	1	0	13	31	1	32
Arkansas	2	3	1	1	0	1	2	0	1	0	11	15	8	23
California	12	8	13	9	13	12	7	14	9	10	107	406	82	488
Colorado	3	2	4	0	1	2	2	0	0	0	14	17	2	19
Connecticut	1	6	0	10	1	0	1	3	1	1	24	38	8	46
Delaware	1	5	0	0	0	0	0	0	0	0	6	6	0	6
Dist. of Columbia	1	2	3	1	5	1	0	3	0	0	16	24	13	37
Florida	4	12	4	3	3	1	5	3	4	12	51	115	41	160
Georgia	4	4	0	6	1	1	1	4	3	3	27	46	21	67
Guam	0	2	0	1	0	0	0	1	0	0	4	4	0	4
Hawaii	0	0	2	1	0	1	0	0	0	0	4	7	0	7
Idaho	3	0	0	0	1	0	0	0	0	0	4	6	3	9
Illinois	19	23	17	16	14	12	5	10	12	6	134	234	41	275
Indiana	4	6	0	1	4	0	1	2	5	0	23	38	8	46
Iowa	4	8	4	2	2	2	0	1	0	1	24	34	2	36
Kansas	5	3	2	1	0	1	0	1	0	1	14	17	3	20
Kentucky	0	1	2	0	1	1	1	1	4	1	12	20	6	26
Louisiana	3	3	3	1	2	4	4	0	1	2	23	61	24	85
Maine	1	1	1	0	0	1	0	1	0	0	5	6	4	10
Maryland	2	1	3	2	1	1	2	0	2	2	16	34	14	48
Massachusetts	4	4	2	4	6	3	6	1	4	0	34	83	75	158
Michigan	4	2	18	7	7	1	27	19	9	2	96	140	64	204
Minnesota	3	4	1	2	0	2	3	0	1	2	18	26	6	32
Mississippi	1	1	0	0	0	3	6	3	4	3	21	26	7	33
Missouri	2	2	2	5	1	2	5	3	3	1	26	56	12	68
Montana	3	2	1	0	0	0	0	1	1	0	8	91	0	91
Nebraska	1	2	1	0	0	0	1	5	1	0	11	16	2	18
Nevada	5	3	1	0	0	1	0	1	0	1	12	25	6	31
New Hampshire	0	2	1	1	0	1	0	2	0	1	8	8	0	8
New Jersey	6	6	5	2	1	0	173	1	0	2	196	212	37	249
New Mexico	0	1	4	1	0	0	0	1	1	1	9	13	7	20
New York	33	39	34	21	29	15	15	14	14	13	227	367	185	552
North Carolina	9	21	5	2	6	3	5	2	3	3	59	76	26	102
North Dakota	1	0	0	0	0	1	0	0	0	2	4	6	0	6
Ohio	10	6	10	2	2	7	8	4	17	9	75	116	27	143
Oklahoma	5	2	3	1	3	2	18	4	1	2	48	66	7	73
Oregon	16	2	4	1	3	2	4	2	0	2	36	47	6	53
Pennsylvania	150	403	112	54	2	6	2	2	0	2	733	829	22	851
Puerto Rico	3	0	0	0	1	0	0	1	1	0	6	6	0	6
Rhode Island	0	0	1	0	1	2	1	0	0	0	5	9	0	9
South Carolina	1	1	2	3	1	1	1	2	1	0	13	19	38	57
South Dakota	0	1	0	0	0	0	0	0	1	1	3	7	0	7
Tennessee	4	6	3	2	2	2	1	2	1	5	28	38	3	41
Texas	134	74	61	12	16	18	12	20	15	9	371	490	27	517
Utah	1	1	3	0	1	1	0	1	0	2	10	19	2	21
Vermont	0	1	0	2	0	0	0	0	0	0	3	4	2	6
Virgin Islands	0	0	0	0	0	0	0	2	0	0	2	2	0	2
Virginia	12	11	3	5	3	4	1	5	3	2	49	77	14	91
Washington	2	9	3	12	4	2	5	4	2	1	44	93	10	103
West Virginia	1	0	2	0	0	0	1	2	4	0	10	19	3	22
Wisconsin	2	9	5	4	1	1	4	8	2	9	45	69	7	76
Wyoming	1	0	1	2	1	1	0	0	0	0	6	6	0	6
U.S. Military	0	4	1	2	2	0	0	2	0	28	39	44	10	54
Totals	484	721	351	206	149	131	333	158	134	142	2809	4313	911	5224

Map 1 — U.S. Map of Total Exonerations for each State (See Table 1's Total column for data.)

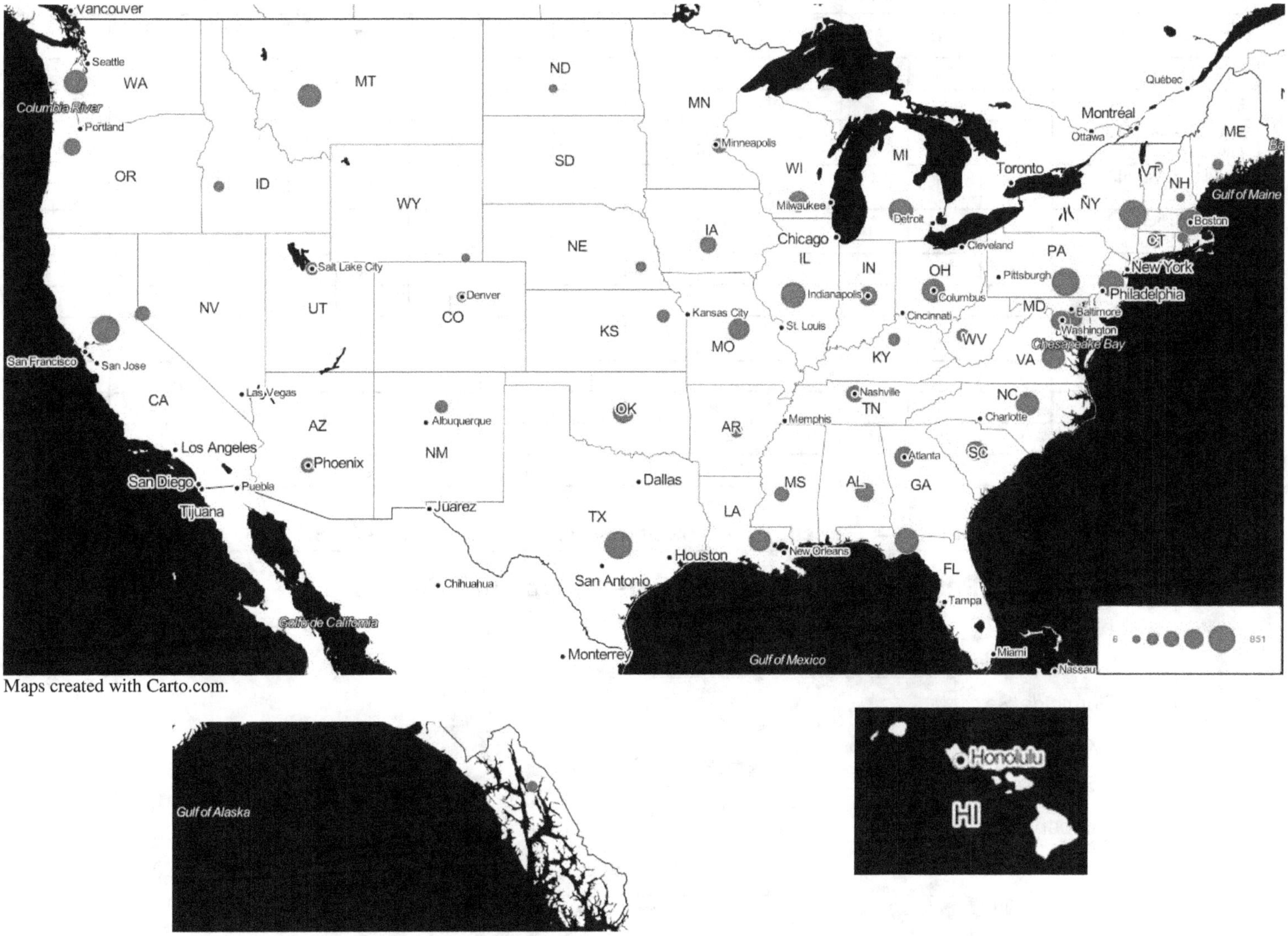

Maps created with Carto.com.

Table 3 — Number of Exonerated People By Jurisdiction (U.S.)														
Jurisdiction	2016	2015	2014	2013	2012	2011	2010	2009	2008	2007	10 yr total	1989-2016	Pre-1989	Total
State case	465	690	323	187	130	117	312	140	107	100	2106	3953	782	4735
Federal case	19	31	28	19	19	14	21	18	28	42	220	360	129	489
Total	484	721	351	206	149	131	333	158	135	142	2809	4313	911	5224

Table 4 — Number of Exonerated People By Sex/Type (U.S.)														
Type	2016	2015	2014	2013	2012	2011	2010	2009	2008	2007	10 yr total	1989-2016	Pre-1989	Total
Male	444	682	312	186	129	118	308	138	120	131	2568	3933	822	4755
Female	40	38	38	20	19	12	24	20	15	11	237	374	69	443
Business	0	1	1	0	1	1	1	0	0	0	5	6	4	10
Unknown	0	0	0	0	0	0	0	0	0	0	0	0	16	16
Total	484	721	351	206	149	131	333	158	135	142	2809	4313	911	5224

Table 5 — Number of Exonerated People By Type of Crime (U.S.)														
Type	2016	2015	2014	2013	2012	2011	2010	2009	2008	2007	10 yr total	1989-2016	Pre-1989	Total
Homicide	59	78	58	49	39	35	37	56	32	27	470	936	428	1364
Homicide/Sex	7	3	2	2	7	6	5	4	3	5	44	90	5	95
Sexual Assault/Rape/Indecent Assault	8	12	16	21	20	16	20	22	20	19	174	382	41	423
Child Sex Assault/Abuse	24	12	9	6	9	11	11	10	12	7	111	214	3	217
Robbery/Theft/Burglary/Extortion	6	13	11	10	8	12	11	12	14	15	112	197	114	311
Assault	9	21	11	2	6	5	5	5	4	7	75	119	9	128
Drug	257	468	170	72	19	13	200	21	17	13	1250	1553	17	1570
Fraud/Forgery/Embezzlement/Bribery	10	17	9	16	9	5	9	9	11	5	100	145	40	185
Child Abuse/Assault	3	1	4	1	0	0	1	1	0	0	11	18	0	18
Violent Other	14	21	17	12	8	2	12	6	12	30	134	172	48	220
Non-violent Other	87	75	44	15	24	26	22	12	10	14	329	487	206	693
Total	484	721	351	206	149	131	333	158	135	142	2809	4313	911	5224

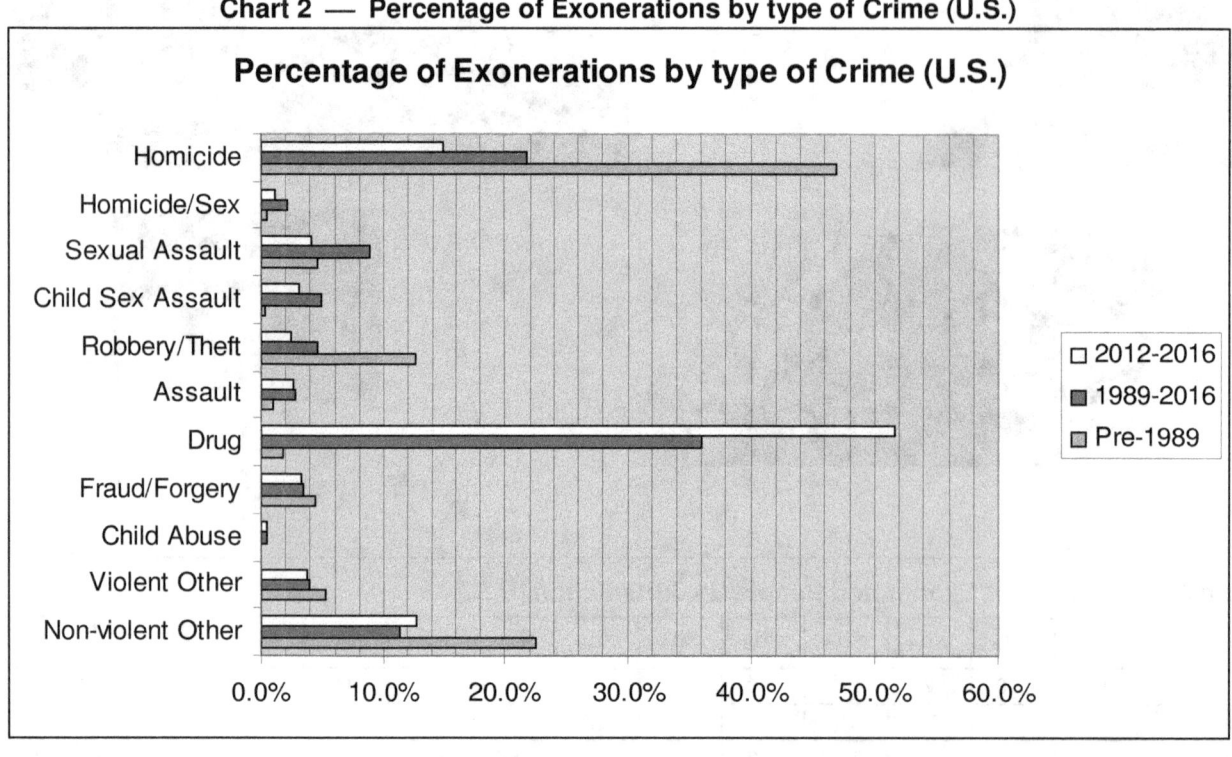

Chart 2 — Percentage of Exonerations by type of Crime (U.S.)

Table 6 — Number of Exonerated People by Race/Ethnicity (U.S.)														
Type	2016	2015	2014	2013	2012	2011	2010	2009	2008	2007	10 yr total	1989-2016	Pre-1989	Total
White	75	94	79	56	50	45	45	52	48	39	583	1145	448	1593
Black	101	108	84	54	53	51	54	54	42	62	663	1111	185	1296
Hispanic	21	26	19	9	17	8	7	8	6	14	135	262	24	286
Asian	2	4	2	1	0	1	1	1	0	0	12	18	6	24
Native American	1	8	0	1	0	0	1	0	0	0	11	16	2	18
Middle eastern roots	1	0	1	0	0	0	0	0	0	0	2	2	0	2
Black/Asian	0	0	0	0	0	0	0	0	0	0	0	1	0	1
Other	1	2	4	0	0	1	1	1	0	0	10	15	0	15
Unidentified	282	479	162	85	29	25	224	42	39	27	1394	1743	246	1989
Total	484	721	351	206	149	131	333	158	135	142	2809	4313	911	5224

Table 7 — Number of Exonerated People By Primary Types of Exculpatory Evidence* (U.S.)														
Type	2016	2015	2014	2013	2012	2011	2010	2009	2008	2007	10 yr Total	1989-2016	Pre-1989	Total
No crime occurred	360	590	219	103	45	33	219	43	42	38	1692	2123	256	2379
Insufficient evidence	95	119	36	20	23	21	27	23	31	20	415	498	185	683
New forensic evidence (DNA & other)	113	87	70	20	32	29	29	30	26	16	452	630	27	657
Prosecution concealment of evidence	193	425	124	76	13	16	197	35	7	33	1119	1417	53	1470
Prosecution fabricated evidence	166	407	115	59	1	8	190	4	2	2	954	1185	12	1197
New witness evidence	21	16	10	8	6	3	7	4	3	5	83	135	60	195
Recantation by accuser	37	14	15	3	6	16	10	8	4	7	120	170	40	210
New DNA evidence**	17	12	8	11	18	22	18	22	17	19	164	360	0	360
Confession by perpetrator	9	5	6	4	5	3	2	4	6	3	47	115	94	209
CCTV, Electronic, or Photographic evidence	8	13	5	4	3	2	0	0	1	1	38	48	0	48

* More than one can apply to a particular case
** Does not include cases where DNA was contributory evidence

Table 8 — Number of Exonerated People By Conviction Method (U.S.)														
Type	2016	2015	2014	2013	2012	2011	2010	2009	2008	2007	10 yr total	1989-2016	Pre-1989	Total
Jury trial	143	166	108	103	89	82	96	98	87	98	1070	1701	534	2235
Judge (Bench trial)	33	63	30	11	11	12	10	12	11	16	209	245	92	337
Guilty Plea	302	488	175	72	25	13	185	10	20	4	1294	1407	23	1430
Alford Plea	6	4	4	0	3	1	5	1	2	1	27	42	2	44
Unidentified	0	0	34	20	21	23	37	37	15	23	209	918	260	1178
Total	484	721	351	206	149	131	333	158	135	142	2809	4313	911	5224

Table 9 — Number of Exonerated People Convicted After More Than One Trial (U.S.)														
Type	2016	2015	2014	2013	2012	2011	2010	2009	2008	2007	10 yr total	1989-2016	Pre-1989	Total
2 trials	12	21	7	7	3	2	3	6	3	5	69	154	80	234
3 trials	1	1	2	3	3	1	1	0	1	1	14	26	17	43
4 trials	2	0	1	1	0	0	0	0	0	0	4	6	1	7
5 trials	0	0	0	0	0	0	0	0	0	0	0	2	3	5
Total	15	22	10	11	6	3	4	6	4	6	87	188	101	289

Table 10 — Number of State Prisoners Exonerated After Federal Habeas Granted (U.S.)														
Year	2016	2015	2014	2013	2012	2011	2010	2009	2008	2007	10 yr total	1989-2016	Pre-1989	Total
Number	6	7	3	4	2	2	4	6	4	7	47	90	36	126

Table 11 — Number of Exonerated People Convicted By Primary Types of Prosecution Evidence* (U.S)													
Type	2016	2015	2014	2013	2012	2011	2010	2009	2008	2007	10 yr total	1989-2016	Pre-1989	Total
Eyewitness error	28	39	41	32	25	28	32	25	51	38	311	656	222	878
Victim ID error	38	33	24	21	22	18	21	13	18	19	189	365	62	427
Informant evidence	18	14	10	4	2	11	6	12	3	7	69	164	51	215
Expert witness	23	14	5	4	12	8	10	10	11	6	80	216	16	232
Judge's Errors	67	95	37	22	24	12	18	22	21	15	266	413	144	557
Police Misconduct/Perjury	194	427	132	72	20	22	201	17	9	9	909	1411	66	1477
Prosecutor Misconduct	37	31	24	20	14	12	12	14	8	33	168	353	73	426
False Confession	13	27	22	9	11	11	18	13	26	8	145	292	73	365
Co-defendant falsely confessed (Defendant didn't confess)	0	1	0	0	0	1	0	0	0	0	2	55	9	64
Concealed evidence	186	422	124	77	14	4	182	16	6	35	880	1394	63	1457
Circumstantial evidence	40	39	36	11	7	8	9	9	3	5	127	218	149	367
Drug analysis (erroneous)	83	52	47	0	1	0	0	1	0	0	101	185	0	185

* More than one can apply to a particular case

Table 12 — Number of Exonerated People By Method of Exoneration (U.S.)													
Type	2016	2015	2014	2013	2012	2011	2010	2009	2008	2007	10 yr total	1989-2016	Pre-1989	Total
Acquitted by Court	113	140	92	36	28	27	28	25	10	46	545	633	217	850
Acquitted after Retrial	14	19	9	11	8	4	9	5	5	9	93	199	73	272
Charges dismissed	355	558	248	156	112	2	294	118	117	83	2139	3283	485	3768
Pardoned	2	4	2	3	1	2	2	10	3	4	33	198	136	334
Total	484	721	351	206	149	131	333	158	135	142	2810	4313	911	5224

Table 13 — Number of Exonerated Persons Involved In A Case With A Co-Defendant (U.S.)													
Type	2016	2015	2014	2013	2012	2011	2010	2009	2008	2007	10 yr total	1989-2016	Pre-1989	Total
2 Co-defendants	22	13	29	8	11	12	8	25	14	16	136	318	95	413
3 Co-defendants	7	12	3	7	6	4	6	4	4	4	50	90	35	125
4 Co-defendants	6	8	3	8	4	1	0	2	0	1	27	63	21	84
5 Co-defendants	0	3	0	8	3	6	0	0	0	0	20	39	22	61
6 Co-defendants	0	0	0	0	0	0	0	5	1	0	6	6	12	18
7 Co-defendants	1	0	3	3	0	0	0	0	0	0	6	14	14	28
9 Co-defendants	0	9	0	3	0	0	0	0	0	0	12	12	15	27
10 Co-defendants	0	10	0	0	0	0	0	0	0	0	10	10	10	20
12 Co-defendants	0	0	0	0	0	0	0	0	0	0	0	0	18	18
14 Co-defendants	0	0	0	0	0	0	0	0	0	0	0	0	14	14
16 Co-defendants	0	0	0	0	0	0	0	0	0	0	0	0	16	16
17 Co-defendants	0	0	0	0	0	0	0	0	0	0	0	0	17	17
24 Co-defendants	0	0	0	0	0	0	0	0	0	0	0	0	48	48
28 Co-defendants	0	0	0	0	0	0	0	0	0	28	28	28	0	28
Total	36	55	38	37	24	23	14	36	19	49	295	580	337	917

Table 14 — Number of Exonerations Involving DNA Evidence By Year				
	U.S.	U.S.		International
Year	Primary Evidence	Contributory Evidence*	US Total	All DNA Evidence*
2016	17	2	19	1
2015	12	6	18	1
2014	8	13	21	2
2013	11	3	14	1
2012	18	3	21	2
2011	22	4	26	3
2010	18	3	21	1
2009	22	5	27	5
2008	17	3	20	4
2007	19	0	19	0
2006	19	2	21	0
2005	17	4	21	1
2004	13	1	14	5
2003	21	3	24	1
2002	23	0	23	1
2001	20	0	20	2
2000	15	1	16	2
1999	13	0	13	1
1998	4	0	4	3
1997	8	1	9	1
1996	14	3	17	0
1995	7	1	8	1
1994	8	3	11	0
1993	4	1	5	0
1992	5	1	6	1
1991	3	0	3	0
1990	1	0	1	0
1989	1	0	1	0
Total	360	63	423	39

* All international cases involved DNA as primary evidence.
** Contributory DNA evidence was insufficient to be relied on to exonerate the person, however, when combined with other exculpatory evidence it contributed to the person's exoneration.

Chart 3 — Exonerations Relying On DNA Evidence in the U.S. and Internationally

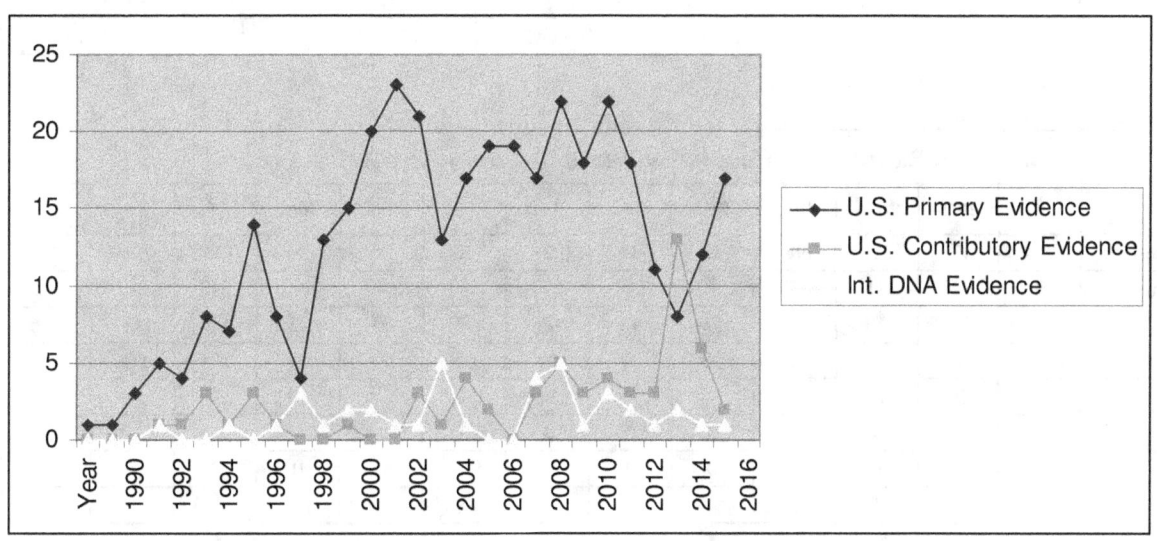

Chart 4 — Percentage of Exonerations based on DNA evidence – 1989-2006 (U.S.)

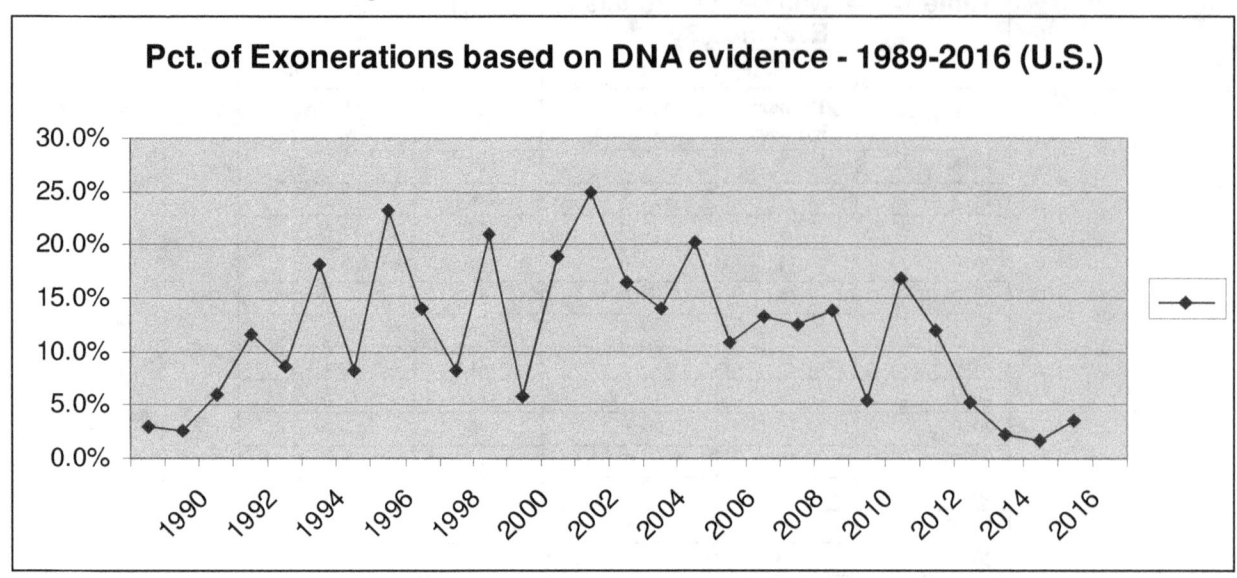

Pct. of Exonerations based on DNA evidence - 1989-2016 (U.S.)

Table 15 — Number of Exonerated People Aided By Conviction Integrity Unit (U.S.)										
Jurisdiction	2016	2015	2014	2013	2012	2011	2010	2009	2008	Total
Harris County, TX	79	48	46	0	0	0	2	1	0	176
Dallas County, TX	0	0	3	0	6	4	1	6	9	29
Kings County, NY	4	7	10	0	0	0	0	0	0	21
Cook County, IL	8	3	3	4	2	0	0	0	0	20
Bexar County, TX	7	2	0	0	0	0	0	0	0	9
Cuyahoga County, OH	7	0	0	0	0	0	0	0	0	7
Multnomah County, OR	5	0	0	0	0	0	0	0	0	5
New York County, NY	0	0	0	1	3	0	0	0	0	4
Baltimore, MD	1	0	3	0	0	0	0	0	0	4
Tarrant County, TX	4	0								4
Lake County, Illinois	0	2	0	0	0	0	0	0	0	2
Philadelphia County, PA	2	0	0	0	0	0	0	0	0	4
Santa Clara County, CA	0	0	0	0	1	0	0	0	0	1
Orleans Parish, Louisiana	0	1	0	0	0	0	0	0	0	1
Ventura County, CA	0	1	0	0	0	0	0	0	0	1
Bronx County, NY	1	0	0	0	0	0	0	0	0	1
Broward County, TX	0	0	0	0	0	0	0	0	0	1
Total	118	64	65	5	12	4	3	7	9	287

Table 16 — Number of Exonerated People By Years In Custody (U.S.)														
Years	2016	2015	2014	2013	2012	2011	2010	2009	2008	2007	10 yr total	1989-2016	Pre-1989	Total
Probation/Fine	314	521	210	98	42	37	221	53	36	56	1587	2059	297	2356
Less than 1 yr	58	68	41	13	8	7	7	3	4	9	218	287	72	359
1 to 9 yrs	58	76	43	44	55	42	66	43	53	43	523	1131	446	1577
10 to 19 yrs	19	24	34	32	30	27	24	38	23	24	275	562	70	632
20 to 29 yrs	34	26	14	16	12	18	12	19	18	10	179	241	21	262
30 to 39 yrs	1	6	9	3	2	0	3	2	1	0	27	32	5	37
40 and greater	0	0	0	0	0	0	0	0	0	0	0	1	0	1
Total	484	721	351	206	149	131	333	158	135	142	2810	4313	911	5224

Table 17 — Average Years Exonerated Person Was In Custody Before Release (All types of cases)

Years	2016	2015	2014	2013	2012	2011	2010	2009	2008	2007	10 yr average	1989-2015	Pre-1989	Total Avg.
United States														
Men	8.7	7.8	10.5	11.3	10.2	11.1	9.1	12.8	10.1	9.4	9.8	9.2	5.2	8.3
Women	2.5	4.4	4.4	3.0	5.3	5.3	5.7	5.0	5.9	2.2	4.2	4.7	3.0	4.5
Combined	8.1	7.5	9.6	10.6	9.7	10.8	8.9	11.9	9.8	8.7	9.3	8.8	5.1	8.0
International														
Men	6.3	5.7	3.7	5.2	6.4	4.6	6.4	4.8	3.2	3.6	4.9	5.5	4.7	5.4
Women	5.5	2.6	1.0	1.5	3.9	7.8	2.3	1.1	1.0	6.1	3.2	3.6	3.5	3.5
Combined	6.2	5.1	3.4	4.9	6.2	4.8	5.9	4.5	3.0	3.8	4.8	5.3	3.1	5.0

Table 18 — Average Years Exonerated Person Was In Custody Before Release (Homicide or Sexual Assault only)

Years	2016	2015	2014	2013	2012	2011	2010	2009	2008	2007	10 yr average	1989-2016	Pre-1989	Total Avg.
United States														
Men	17.7	15.6	17.7	16.2	14.1	15.9	13.9	15.4	15.3	11.9	15.5	12.9	6.3	11.2
Women	7.3	14.7	11.5	5.4	9.9	9.3	12.5	5.7	9.0	2.3	8.6	7.6	3.8	7.0
Combined	17.1	15.6	17.1	15.3	13.7	15.7	13.8	14.4	15.0	11.1	15.0	12.6	6.2	11.0
International														
Men	9.2	7.9	4.6	9.2	7.4	6.3	10.7	7.0	3.8	5.5	6.9	7.4	6.5	7.3
Women	7.9	4.5	4.1	2.1	5.6	7.8	2.4	2.1	1.4	6.4	4.9	5.3	4.6	5.2
Combined	9.1	7.4	4.6	8.3	7.3	6.5	8.9	6.8	3.7	5.6	6.7	7.2	6.3	7.1

Table 19 — Average Years Exonerated Person Was In Custody Before Release (Non-Homicide or Sexual Assault only)

Years	2016	2015	2014	2013	2012	2011	2010	2009	2008	2007	10 yr average	1989-2016	Pre-1989	Total Avg.
United States														
Men	2.7	2.4	3.6	3.4	4.7	5.5	4.9	6.1	4.5	6.2	3.9	4.0	2.5	3.8
Women	0.7	0.8	1.3	0.7	2.0	2.6	2.2	4.0	3.6	2.0	1.6	2.8	2.0	2.7
Combined	2.5	2.2	3.2	3.1	4.3	5.3	4.7	5.8	4.5	5.7	3.6	3.9	2.6	3.6
International														
Men	1.4	2.0	1.8	2.4	5.7	2.6	2.6	2.4	2.4	1.9	2.7	2.9	3.0	2.9
Women	1.8	0.8	1.0	0.2	2.7	0.0	2.0	0.6	0.8	5.3	1.4	1.5	2.5	1.6
Combined	1.5	1.8	1.6	2.3	5.5	2.6	2.6	2.2	2.3	2.1	2.6	2.8	1.7	2.6

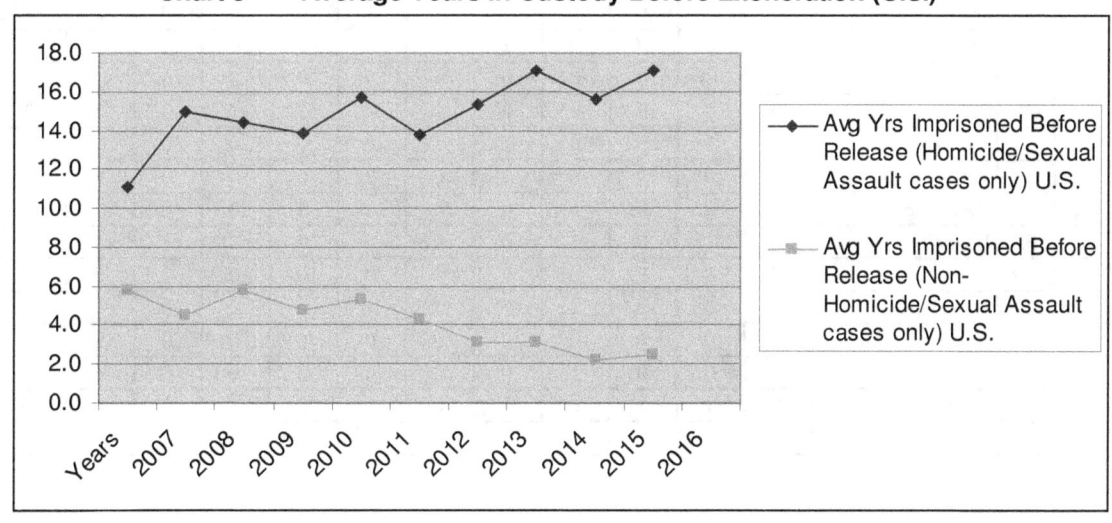

Chart 5 — Average Years in Custody Before Exoneration (U.S.)

Table 20 — Number of Exonerated People By County (12 or more) (U.S.)															
County/Parish/Borough	State	Major City	2016	2015	2014	2013	2012	2011	2010	2009	2008	2007	10 yr total	1989-2015	Pre-1989	Total
Philadelphia	PA	Philadelphia	146	397	110	53	0	2	1	0	0	0	709	770	10	780
Los Angeles	CA	Los Angeles	1	1	4	4	8	6	2	8	3	5	42	248	47	295
Harris	TX	Houston	80	53	47	3	4	1	4	3	1	1	197	212	3	215
Cook	IL	Chicago	13	5	13	11	10	11	4	7	6	4	84	156	25	181
Camden	NJ	Camden	0	1	0	0	0	0	172	0	0	0	173	174	3	177
New York (Manhattan)	NY	New York City	3	11	5	5	7	5	0	3	6	1	46	68	56	124
Kings (Brooklyn)	NY	New York City	8	15	1	5	2	1	3	1	1	4	55	90	24	114
Wayne	MI	Detroit	3	0	5	4	1	0	6	2	3	0	24	44	32	76
Bronx	NY	New York City	2	0	4	6	2	3	3	1	0	2	23	47	14	61
Suffolk	MA	Boston	1	0	1	0	0	0	0	0	2	0	4	25	26	51
Queens	NY	New York City	2	2	1	1	2	4	2	1	0	2	17	35	13	48
Tulsa	OK	Tulsa	2	0	2	0	1	7	17	2	0	0	31	39	0	39
Swisher	TX	Tulia	0	1	0	0	0	2	0	0	0	0	3	38	0	38
Cuyahoga	OH	Cleveland	10	1	5	0	1	5	2	1	1	1	27	32	5	37
Essex	MA	Salem	0	1	0	0	0	1	0	0	0	0	2	9	27	36
District of Columbia	DC	District of Columbia	1	2	3	1	5	1	0	3	0	0	16	24	11	35
Suffolk	NY	Southhampton	2	2	0	1	7	1	0	1	2	0	16	22	11	33
King	WA	Seattle	1	1	0	1	0	0	1	2	0	0	6	20	7	27
Orleans	LA	New Orleans	2	1	1	1	2	1	0	0	0	0	8	24	2	26
Kern	CA	Bakersfield	1	0	0	0	0	0	0	0	0	0	1	1	24	25
Charleston	SC	Charleston	0	0	0	0	0	1	0	0	1	0	2	25	0	25
Milwaukee	WI	Milwaukee	1	2	0	0	0	0	2	6	0	3	14	24	0	24
San Diego	CA	San Diego	0	0	3	0	1	3	0	1	1	0	10	22	1	23
Monroe	NY	Rochester	2	2	1	1	1	0	2	0	0	0	8	12	11	23
Miami-Dade	FL	Miami	1	2	0	0	0	1	0	0	3	0	7	13	10	23
Richmond	VA	Richmond	7	8	0	0	0	1	0	2	0	0	18	22	1	23
Broward	FL	Fort Lauderdale	1	3	0	0	1	0	1	1	0	2	9	17	5	22
Erie	NY	Buffalo	1	2	1	0	0	0	2	1	1	2	11	13	8	21
Montgomery	TX	Conroe	8	5	1	1	0	2	0	0	0	0	18	21	0	21
Middlesex	MA	Lowell	2	1	0	2	0	0	0	1	0	0	5	13	7	20
East Baton Rouge	LA	Baton Rouge	0	0	0	1	0	0	0	0	0	0	0	1	18	19
Richland	OH	Mansfield	0	1	1	0	0	0	0	0	14	2	18	18	0	18
Oakland	MI	Oak Park	0	0	3	0	1	0	4	1	1	0	12	14	4	18
Berrien	IN	Benton Harbor	0	0	0	2	0	0	1	14	0	0	15	17	0	17
Santa Clara	CA	Cupertino	0	1	0	0	1	0	1	1	1	2	7	16	0	16
Clark	NV	Las Vegas	3	0	1	0	0	1	0	1	0	1	7	13	3	16
Maricopa	AZ	Phoenix	1	1	0	0	2	0	2	0	1	0	7	15	1	16
Jefferson	AL	Birmingham	0	2	0	0	1	2	0	0	0	0	5	16	0	16
Oklahoma	OK	Oklahoma City	2	1	0	1	0	1	0	2	0	2	9	13	3	16
San Francisco	CA	San Francisco	0	2	0	0	0	1	2	0	0	0	5	8	8	16
Allegheny	PA	Pittsburgh	1	0	0	0	1	1	0	0	0	0	3	14	1	15
York	NC	Rock Hill	0	14	0	0	0	0	0	0	0	0	14	14	0	14
Franklin	OH	Columbus	0	0	0	0	0	0	1	1	0	0	2	9	5	14
Bexar	TX	San Antonio	8	3	0	0	1	1	0	0	0	0	13	13	1	14
Orange	CA	Santa Ana	1	0	2	0	1	0	2	0	0	0	6	13	0	13
New Haven	CT	New Haven	0	3	0	4	0	0	1	2	0	0	10	12	1	13
Hillsborough	FL	Tampa	0	1	0	1	0	0	0	0	0	2	4	11	2	13
Multnomah	OR	Portland	5	0	2	0	0	0	0	0	0	1	8	12	1	13
Hampden	MA	Springfield	0	0	0	2	3	1	1	0	0	0	7	10	3	13
Chelan	WA	Wenatchee	0	0	0	0	0	0	0	0	0	0	0	12	0	12
Macomb	MI	Michigan	0	0	0	1	0	0	4	0	0	1	6	11	1	12
Travis	TX	Austin	0	1	1	0	1	0	0	2	1	0	5	12	0	12
Tarrant	TX	Fort Worth	6	0	0	0	1	0	0	1	0	0	8	12	0	12

Table 21 — Number of Exonerated People By Country – International Cases Only														
Country	2016	2015	2014	2013	2012	2011	2010	2009	2008	2007	10 yr total	1989-2016	Pre-1989	Total
Afghanistan	0	0	0	0	0	0	1	0	0	0	1	1	0	1
Angola	0	0	0	0	0	18	0	0	0	0	18	18	0	18
Australia	14	10	11	16	8	12	6	11	22	6	116	154	16	170
Bahamas	1	5	0	2	0	1	0	0	0	0	9	9	0	9
Bahrain	0	0	0	0	9	0	0	0	1	1	11	12	0	12
Bangladesh	0	3	0	0	0	0	0	1	0	0	4	4	0	4
Barbados	2	0	0	0	0	0	0	0	0	0	2	2	1	3
Belarus	0	0	0	0	0	0	3	0	0	0	3	3	0	3
Belgium	0	0	0	0	0	0	0	0	7	0	7	7	0	7
Belize	0	2	0	0	0	0	1	4	0	0	7	9	0	9
Bermuda	1	2	0	2	0	0	0	0	0	0	5	6	0	6
Bhutan	2	0	0	0	0	0	0	0	0	0	2	2	0	2
Botswana	0	0	0	0	0	0	0	0	2	0	2	2	0	2
Brazil	0	1	0	0	0	0	0	0	0	0	1	1	0	1
Brunei Darussalam	0	0	0	0	0	0	0	0	1	0	1	1	0	1
Bulgaria	0	0	0	0	0	0	0	1	0	0	1	1	0	1
Cambodia	0	0	0	1	0	0	0	0	0	0	1	1	0	1
Canada	6	8	4	2	5	4	7	6	9	8	59	98	6	104
Cayman Islands	0	0	0	1	0	3	1	1	0	0	6	6	0	6
Chile	0	0	0	0	0	0	0	0	0	0	0	3	0	3
China	11	6	2	2	2	0	3	0	0	0	26	31	0	31
Colombia	0	1	0	1	0	0	0	0	1	0	3	3	0	3
Costa Rica	0	6	0	1	0	0	0	0	0	0	7	8	0	8
Croatia	1	0	0	0	2	0	0	0	0	0	3	7	0	7
Cuba	0	0	0	0	0	0	1	0	0	0	1	1	0	1
Cyprus	0	0	0	0	0	0	0	0	0	3	3	3	0	3
Czech Republic	0	0	0	0	0	4	0	0	0	0	4	4	0	4
Denmark	0	0	0	0	0	0	0	0	0	0	0	1	0	1
Egypt	7	12	0	0	0	0	2	1	0	0	22	23	0	23
Fiji	0	1	0	4	2	5	0	0	5	0	17	17	0	17
Finland	4	1	0	0	0	1	0	0	0	0	6	6	0	6
France	0	1	3	0	2	1	0	6	0	0	13	20	7	27
Germany	0	0	0	0	2	0	0	1	0	2	5	16	27	43
Ghana	1	4	0	0	0	1	0	2	0	2	10	11	0	11
Greece	1	0	0	0	0	12	0	0	0	1	14	15	0	15
Guatemala	0	0	0	0	0	0	0	0	0	0	0	0	3	3
Hong Kong	5	2	6	6	2	7	1	2	0	5	36	36	0	36
Hungary	0	0	0	0	0	1	0	0	0	0	1	3	0	3
India	32	40	18	18	52	6	4	4	3	2	179	186	6	192
Indonesia	0	0	0	0	0	0	0	1	3	0	4	7	0	7
Iran	0	0	3	0	0	0	0	0	1	0	4	4	0	4
Ireland	2	5	3	0	0	0	1	1	1	0	13	26	3	29
Isle of Man	0	0	1	0	0	0	0	0	0	0	1	1	0	1
Israel	1	1	16	0	0	0	1	1	0	0	20	28	1	29
Italy	3	8	16	0	3	1	2	1	0	1	35	37	1	38
Jamaica	0	0	0	0	3	1	0	7	3	0	14	19	5	24
Japan	3	2	1	0	1	2	2	0	1	1	13	16	10	26
Jersey	0	0	0	0	0	0	0	1	0	0	1	1	0	1
Kenya	0	1	6	0	3	4	0	4	2	4	24	26	0	26
Kosovo	0	0	0	0	0	0	0	1	0	0	1	1	0	1
Kuwait	1	0	0	0	0	0	0	0	0	0	1	2	0	2
Latvia	0	0	0	0	0	0	0	0	0	1	1	1	0	1
Libya	0	0	0	2	0	0	0	0	0	6	8	8	0	8
Lithuania	0	0	0	1	0	0	0	0	0	0	1	1	0	1
Malawi	19	0	0	0	0	0	0	0	0	2	21	22	0	22
Malaysia	4	2	7	2	0	0	2	3	7	2	29	34	0	34
Maldives	0	0	0	2	0	0	0	0	0	0	2	2	0	2
Malta	7	0	0	0	0	0	0	0	0	0	7	7	0	7

Country	2016	2015	2014	2013	2012	2011	2010	2009	2008	2007	10 yr total	1989-2016	Pre-1989	Total
Mauritius	1	0	0	0	0	0	0	0	0	0	1	1	0	1
Mexico	0	1	0	1	1	0	0	0	0	0	3	9	0	9
Mongolia	0	3	0	0	0	0	0	0	0	0	3	3	0	3
Morocco	0	0	1	0	0	0	0	0	1	0	2	2	0	2
Namibia	0	0	2	1	1	0	0	0	0	0	4	5	0	5
Nauru	0	0	0	0	0	0	0	0	0	0	0	0	1	1
Netherlands	0	0	0	0	0	0	2	1	0	0	3	6	1	7
Netherlands (Dutch) Antilles	0	0	0	2	0	0	0	0	0	0	2	2	0	2
New Caledonia	0	0	0	0	0	0	0	1	0	0	1	1	0	1
New Zealand	7	13	11	4	0	2	4	4	11	5	61	72	2	74
Nicaragua	0	0	0	0	0	0	0	0	0	1	1	1	0	1
Nigeria	0	3	0	3	1	2	0	0	0	0	9	16	1	17
North Korea	0	0	0	0	0	0	0	2	0	0	2	2	0	2
Northern Mariana Islands	0	1	1	1	0	0	0	0	0	0	3	3	0	3
Norway	0	0	0	0	0	0	0	11	13	18	42	70	0	70
Pakistan	2	9	0	0	2	0	0	1	0	0	14	23	0	23
Peru	2	0	0	0	1	0	1	0	0	0	4	4	0	4
Philippines	1	1	0	0	0	0	7	1	0	0	10	10	1	11
Poland	0	0	0	0	0	0	0	0	0	0	0	1	0	1
Portugal	1	0	0	0	0	0	0	0	0	0	1	1	0	1
Qatar	0	0	2	0	0	0	0	0	0	0	2	2	0	2
Russian Federation	0	0	0	1	0	0	0	0	0	0	1	2	15	17
Rwanda	0	0	0	0	0	0	0	0	1	0	1	1	0	1
Saint Kitts and Nevis	0	1	0	1	0	0	1	4	4	1	12	12	0	12
Saint Lucia	0	0	0	0	0	0	0	0	0	1	1	1	0	1
Saudi Arabia	0	0	0	0	0	0	0	0	0	0	0	7	0	7
Senegal	0	0	0	0	0	0	0	9	0	0	9	9	0	9
Serbia	0	1	0	1	0	0	2	1	0	0	5	5	0	5
Seychelles	0	0	0	0	0	0	0	0	0	0	0	0	1	1
Sierra Leone	0	0	0	1	0	1	0	0	0	0	2	2	0	2
Singapore	0	0	1	2	3	0	0	1	2	0	9	10	1	11
Somalia	0	0	0	2	0	0	0	0	0	0	2	2	0	2
South Africa	1	3	2	0	1	0	0	0	6	2	15	30	2	32
South Korea	4	0	0	1	0	0	0	0	3	8	16	17	0	17
Spain	0	0	1	0	0	5	0	0	4	0	10	16	0	16
Sri Lanka	0	0	0	0	0	0	0	1	0	0	1	1	1	2
Sudan	0	1	1	0	0	0	0	0	0	4	6	6	0	6
Swaziland	0	0	0	1	0	0	0	0	0	0	1	1	0	1
Sweden	5	0	1	2	4	1	1	0	2	0	16	19	0	19
Switzerland	1	0	0	0	0	0	1	2	0	0	4	5	0	5
Taiwan	1	0	0	0	0	2	0	0	0	0	3	3	0	3
Tanzania	1	2	13	1	1	0	0	1	1	12	32	33	0	33
Thailand	0	0	0	0	0	0	0	0	0	2	2	6	0	6
Tonga	0	0	0	0	0	0	0	1	0	0	1	1	0	1
Trinidad and Tobago	0	0	1	1	0	0	1	5	0	1	9	10	0	10
Tunisia	0	0	0	1	0	0	0	0	0	0	1	1	0	1
Turkey	275	2	1	63	0	0	0	0	0	0	341	344	0	344
Turks and Caicos Islands	0	0	0	0	5	0	0	0	0	0	5	5	0	5
Uganda	1	0	1	0	1	4	1	0	0	1	9	12	0	12
Ukraine	0	0	0	0	0	0	0	0	0	0	0	1	0	1
United Arab Emirates	1	0	0	7	1	5	0	3	0	0	17	18	0	18
United Kingdom (Great Britain)	25	44	65	26	20	53	32	46	42	66	419	855	107	962
U.N. Court in the Hague	1	0	0	0	0	0	0	0	1	0	2	2	0	2
Vanuatu	1	0	0	0	0	0	0	0	0	0	1	2	0	2
Vietnam	0	1	1	1	0	0	0	0	1	0	4	11	1	12
Virgin Islands (British)	0	0	2	0	0	1	0	0	0	1	4	4	0	4
Zambia	0	0	0	2	4	0	1	0	0	0	7	7	0	7
Zimbabwe	3	1	4	0	0	1	4	1	1	2	17	18	0	18
Total	462	211	208	189	142	161	96	155	163	172	1959	2687	220	2907

Table 22 — Number of Exonerated People By Type of Crime (International)														
Type	2016	2015	2014	2013	2012	2011	2010	2009	2008	2007	10 yr total	1989-2016	Pre-1989	Total
Homicide	43	61	50	28	38	29	19	32	41	35	376	617	53	670
Homicide/Sex	1	1	3	3	1	1	7	0	1	2	20	26	1	27
Sexual Assault/Rape/Indecent Assault	9	8	11	9	7	10	14	18	19	28	133	220	3	223
Child Sex Assault/Abuse	7	10	9	3	0	5	5	3	4	3	49	74	1	75
Robbery/Theft/Burglary/Extortion	7	12	9	10	7	8	5	8	10	21	97	168	45	213
Assault	19	13	8	6	3	4	3	24	25	8	113	140	13	153
Drug	2	12	4	8	2	4	7	9	10	19	77	106	4	110
Fraud/Forgery/Embezzlement/Bribery	25	23	4	12	2	10	9	10	7	13	115	143	7	150
Child Abuse/Assault	0	0	2	0	0	0	0	0	0	0	2	6	0	6
Violent Other	290	10	17	11	47	7	11	17	30	9	449	514	54	568
Non-violent Other	59	61	91	99	35	83	16	34	16	34	528	673	39	712
Total	462	211	208	189	142	161	96	155	163	172	1959	2687	220	2907

Table 23 — Number of Exonerated People By Method of Exoneration (International)														
Type	2016	2015	2014	2013	2012	2011	2010	2009	2008	2007	10 yr total	1989-2016	Pre-1989	Total
Acquitted by reviewing Court	433	169	120	122	121	63	35	29	22	42	1156	1212	14	1226
Acquitted after Retrial	9	13	4	7	0	7	6	4	11	14	75	107	15	122
Charges dismissed	20	21	84	59	21	9	4	9	7	1	272	300	2	302
Pardoned	0	8	0	1	0	5	0	1	1	6	22	96	13	109

Table 24 — Number of Exonerated Persons Involved In A Case With A Co-Defendant (International)														
Type	2016	2015	2014	2013	2012	2011	2010	2009	2008	2007	10 yr total	1989-2016	Pre-1989	Total
2 Co-defendants	14	20	28	26	20	5	7	9	18	14	161	234	15	249
3 Co-defendants	9	24	12	3	15	9	11	13	9	12	117	165	30	195
4 Co-defendants	12	4	0	8		16	0	4	16	8	68	98	1	99
5 Co-defendants	10	5	10	0	10	15	0	5	10	5	70	75	5	80
6 Co-defendants	6	6	12	0	0	5	1	0	0	6	36	54	0	54
7 Co-defendants	0	0	14	0	0	0	7	0	7	7	35	35	6	41
8 Co-defendants	8	7	0	0	0	0	0	8	0	8	31	31	0	31
9 Co-defendants	0	0	0	0	9	0	0	9	0	0	18	18	0	18
11 Co-defendants	0	0	0	0	22	0	0	0	0	0	22	22	0	22
12 Co-defendants	0	12	0	0	0	12	0	0	0	0	24	24	0	24
13 Co-defendants	0	0	0	0	0	0	0	0	0	0	0		13	13
16 Co-defendants	0	0	16	0	0	0	0	0	0	0	16	16	0	16
17 Co-defendants	0	0	0	0	17	0	0	0	0	0	17	17	0	17
18 Co-defendants	0	0	0	0	0	18	0	0	0	0	18	18	0	18
19 Co-defendants	19	0	0	0	0	0	0	0	0	0	19	19	0	19
20 Co-defendants	0	0	0	0	0	20	0	0	0	0	20	20	0	20
29 Co-defendants	0	0	29	0	0	0	0	0	0	0	29	29	0	29
Total	78	78	121	37	93	100	26	48	60	60	701	875	70	945

Map 2 — World Map of Total Exonerations for each Country (See Table 21's Total column for data.)

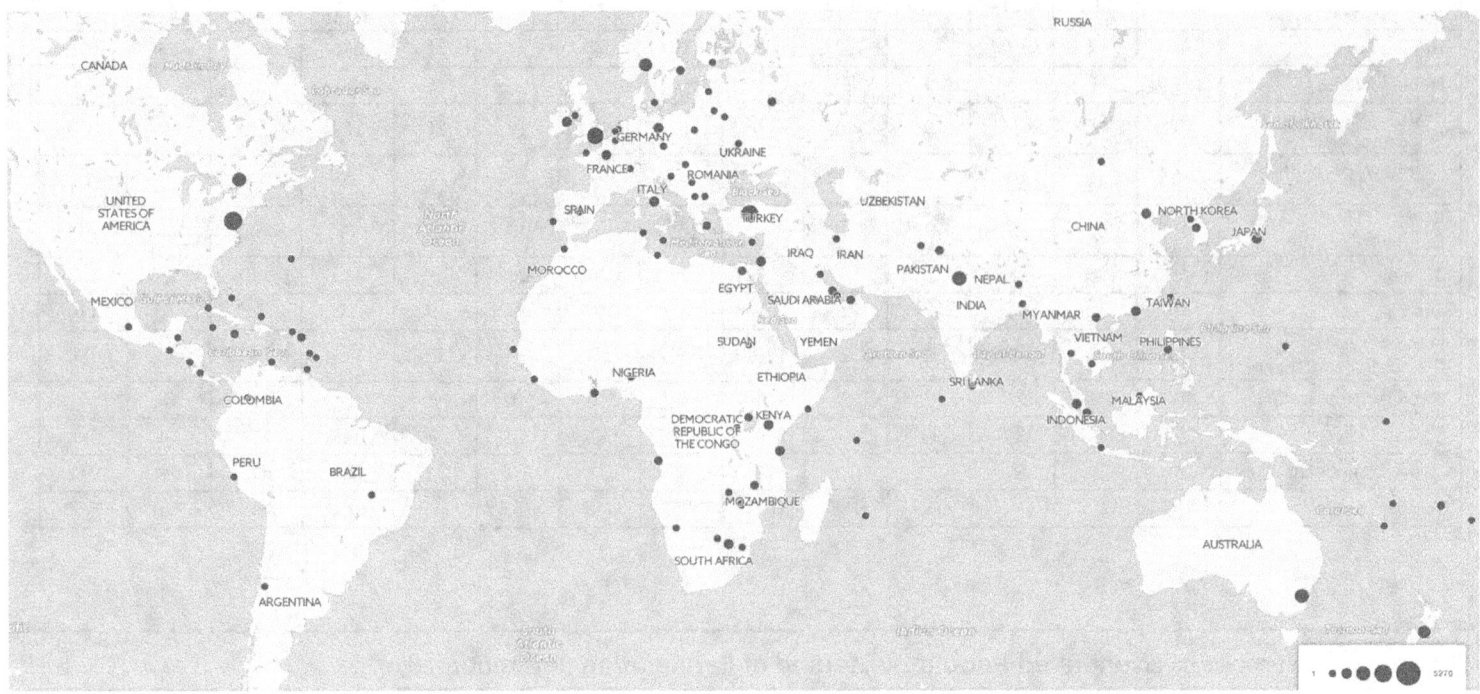

Map created with Carto.com.

Federal Court Is The Death Zone For Innocent State Prisoners[15]

Federal court is the place where an innocent state prisoner goes as a last resort when the highest court in their state has denied justice. It is common to hear people assert a prisoner will finally get justice when they get out of what is viewed as a state court system rigged to protect shady convictions and wrongdoing by prosecutors and police. Federal court is envisioned as nirvana populated with judges dedicated to seeking the truth. Unfortunately, reality is that the overwhelming majority of state prisoners have the last vestige of their belief in justice crushed in federal court.

Six state prisoners were exonerated in 2016 after having their federal habeas corpus petition granted.[16] Six out of the thousands of federal habeas petitions filed each year by state prisoners in the United States, plus Puerto Rico, Guam, and the U.S. Virgin Islands. Those six people were:

- Joel Albert Alcox, convicted of murder and robbery in California. He spent 26 years in custody.
- Jaime Caetano, convicted of possessing a dangerous weapon (stun gun) in Massachusetts. She was jailed for several days.
- Teshome Campbell, convicted of first-degree murder in Illinois. He spent 18 years in custody.
- Jimmie Gardner, convicted of rape and assault in West Virginia. He spent 27 years in custody.
- William Haughey, convicted of arson in New York. He spent 8 years in custody.
- Jules Letemps, convicted of sexual assault and kidnapping in Florida. He spent 27 years in custody.

The exoneration in 2016 of those six after federal court review of their convictions wasn't an anomaly. It was slightly more than the annual average of less than five from 2002 to 2016, when there were a total of 64 exonerations of a state prisoner following the grant of their federal habeas corpus. For each year from 2002 to 2016 the number of exonerations were:

2016 = 6
2015 = 7
2014 = 3
2013 = 4
2012 = 2
2011 = 4
2010 = 4
2009 = 6
2008 = 4
2007 = 7
2006 = 3
2005 = 2
2004 = 3
2003 = 5
2002 = 4
Total = 64

The 64 state prisoner exonerations in the fifteen years from 2002 to 2016 was *less than one* for each of the 94 federal court districts. Those 64 exonerations were of state prisoners in only 20 states, plus the District of Columbia and Puerto Rico:

Arizona = 1
California = 12
Connecticut = 1
District of Columbia = 2
Florida = 2

---

[15] This is a modification of the article by Hans Sherrer, "Federal Court Is The Death Zone For Innocent State Prisoners," published by Justice Denied on February 16, 2017. Available online at, http://justicedenied.org/wordpress/archives/3511 .

[16] Innocents Database, http://forejustice.org/idb1989us.html .

Illinois = 6
Louisiana = 1
Massachusetts = 4
Nevada = 3
New Jersey = 1
New York = 12
North Carolina = 2
Ohio = 6
Oklahoma = 2
Oregon = 1
Pennsylvania = 1
Puerto Rico = 1
Texas = 1
Virginia = 1
Washington = 1
West Virginia = 1
Wisconsin = 2

More than half – 36 – came from federal courts in four states: California (12); Illinois (6); Ohio (6); and, New York (12). *So in the fifteen years from 2002 to 2016 there wasn't a single state prisoner exonerated by a federal court in thirty states*!

The rarity of an exoneration as the result of action by a federal court is not only shown by how few occur, but by the low number of successful petitions compared with the number of habeas petitions filed. From 2002 to 2016 there were 51,010 federal habeas petitions filed by state prisoners seeking to overturn their conviction(s).[17] That means the *overall* success rate was one out of 797, or 00.1255%. That is very long odds at best.

However, federal courts treat a case in which the death penalty was imposed more favorably than a non-death penalty case. That is reflected in the significant difference in the exoneration rate between the two types of cases.

There were 56 exonerations out of the 50,884 state prisoner non-death penalty federal habeas petitions filed. So 1 out of 909 petitions was successful, a rate of 0.11%.

There were 126 habeas petitions filed in a death penalty case, and 8 exonerations. So 1 out of 15.75 petitions was successful, a rate of 6.3%.

Hovering over every failed federal habeas corpus petition is the gleeful ghost of deceased U.S. Supreme Court Chief Justice William Rehnquist. He was a champion of the Anti-Terrorism and Effective Death Penalty Act (AEDPA) enacted in 1996. Rehnquist was a passionate proponent of limiting the ability of state prisoners to successfully raise post-conviction constitutional claims in federal court. The AEDPA codified some of the judicial rules in effect during his reign as chief justice.

The AEDPA established procedural requirements and review standards so onerous that few state prisoners meet them, regardless of the merits of their case – or their factual innocence. Consequently, the AEDPA is working exactly as Rehnquist intended to make federal court the place where unjustly convicted or sentenced state prisoners go to have their hopes die.

Many commentators – including federal appellate court judges – have observed that the AEDPA has had a devastating effect on the ability of a state prisoner – even those who may be actually innocent – to obtain federal habeas relief. In 2015 articles by Alex Kozinski and Stephen Reinhardt, who are both judges on the U.S. Court of Appeals for the Ninth Circuit, explained the negative effect of the AEDPA on state prisoners seeking federal habeas corpus relief.

Judge Stephen Reinhardt wrote in "The Demise of Habeas Corpus and the Rise of Qualified Immunity: The Court's Ever Increasing Limitations on the Development and Enforcement of Constitutional Rights and Some

---

[17] Information source: Statistical Tables for the Federal Judiciary, United States Courts, http://www.uscourts.gov/statistics-reports/analysis-reports/statistical-tables-federal-judiciary . (last viewed March 15, 2017)

Particularly Unfortunate Consequences," 113 *Mich. L.R.* 1219, Issue 7, (2015):

> "The collapse of habeas corpus as a remedy for even the most glaring of constitutional violations ranks among the greater wrongs of our legal era. Once hailed as the Great Writ, and still feted with all the standard rhetorical flourishes, habeas corpus has been transformed over the past two decades from a vital guarantor of liberty into an instrument for ratifying the power of state courts to disregard the protections of the Constitution.
>
> … any participant in our habeas regime would have to agree that it resembles a twisted labyrinth of deliberately crafted legal obstacles that make it as difficult for habeas petitioners to succeed in pursuing the Writ as it would be for a Supreme Court Justice to strike out Babe Ruth, Joe DiMaggio, and Mickey Mantle in succession—even with the Chief Justice calling balls and strikes." (1219-20)

Similarly, Judge Alex Kozinski wrote in, "Criminal Law 2.0," 44 *Geo. L.J.* Ann. Rev. Crim. Proc (2015) (Preface, iii):

> "The federal court safety-value was abruptly dismantled in 1996 when Congress passed and President Clinton signed the Antiterrorism and Effective Death Penalty Act. …
>
> We now regularly have to stand by in impotent silence, even though it may appear to us that an innocent person has been convicted.
>
> AEDPA is a cruel, unjust and unnecessary law that effectively removes federal judges as safeguards against miscarriages of justice. It has resulted and continues to result in much human suffering." (xli-xlii)

The United States Court website has statistical tables regarding the filing of federal habeas petitions.[18]

The information about the exonerated individuals and the number of exonerations is from the Innocents Database.[19]

---

[18] Statistical Tables for the Federal Judiciary, United States Courts, http://www.uscourts.gov/statistics-reports/analysis-reports/statistical-tables-federal-judiciary . (last viewed March 15, 2017)

[19] Innocents Database, http://forejustice.org/exonerations.htm . (last viewed March 15, 2017)

www.ingramcontent.com/pod-product-compliance
Lightning Source LLC
Chambersburg PA
CBHW081316180526
45170CB00007B/2728